WHAT DO YOU KNOW ABOUT

DYSLEXIA
& ASSOCIATED DIFFICULTIES

Pete Sanders and Steve Myers

W
FRANKLIN WATTS
LONDON • SYDNEY

This edition published in 2000
© Aladdin Books Ltd 1996

Designed and produced by
Aladdin Books Ltd
28 Percy Street
London W1P 0LD

First published in
Great Britain in 1996 by
Franklin Watts
96 Leonard Street
London EC2A 4XD

Previously published in
hardcover in the series
Let's Discuss.

ISBN: 0 7496 2223 7 (hardback)
ISBN: 0 7496 3751 X (paperback)

A catalogue record for this
book is available from the
British Library.

Printed in Belgium

Designer   Tessa Barwick
Editor   Sarah Levete
Illustrator   Mike Lacey
Picture research Brooks Krikler
                Research

Pete Sanders is Senior
Lecturer in health education at
the University of North
London. He was a head
teacher for ten years and has
written many books on social
issues for children.

Steve Myers is a freelance
writer. He has co-written titles
in this and other series and
worked on several educational
projects for children.

The consultant, Dr David
Dewhurst, Dip. RSA (spLD),
teaches, assesses and
advises on dyslexia. He was
formerly a Deputy Head
with responsibility for
Special Needs.

Contents

HOW TO USE THIS BOOK

The books in this series are intended to help young people to understand more about personal issues that may affect their lives. Each book can be read alone, or together with a parent, carer, teacher or helper, so that there is an opportunity to talk through ideas as they come up. Issues raised in the storyline are explored in the accompanying text, inviting further discussion.

At the end of the book there is a chapter called "What Can We Do?". This section provides practical ideas which will be useful for both young people and adults, as well as a list of the names and addresses of organisations and helplines, which offer further information and support.

Introduction

We do not all learn at the same pace or in the same way. People who have a difficulty with learning deserve support which will enable them to develop to their full potential.

An important part of life is the ability to learn. But some people have specific difficulties with learning, for which they may need specialised help. Dyslexia is one such difficulty which affects reading, writing and concentration, making it hard for people to learn with the same ease as others. This book helps you to understand more about dyslexia and similar problems. Each chapter introduces a different aspect of the subject, illustrated by a continuing storyline. The characters in the story deal with situations which many young people experience. By the end, you will understand more about dyslexia, how it can affect people's lives, and what can be done to help.

—2— How Do We Learn?

The ways in which we take in knowledge and put it to use may be different for each of us.

Learning is not a single event. It is something which goes on throughout our lives and is more than just knowing facts. Learning is the process by which we gather information, acquire and practise skills and develop our own attitudes and values. Reading, writing and the ability to think clearly are important tools which help us to do this and to live our lives to the full.

From the moment we are born, we begin to learn about the world around us. We do this in a variety of ways. Babies learn by copying what an adult does, repeating the same thing, until they can do it. As we grow older, we are often told what to do, and immediately understand what is necessary. Sometimes you will learn from experience – if you have made a mistake you may realise where you went wrong and know what you need to do next time to get it right. Asking questions can help you to understand issues or facts.

Explaining a process to someone else can also strengthen your own understanding of a subject. Another important part of learning is being able to make links between different ideas. Other people asking you questions which make you think carefully, can help you to make these connections. Drawing on our feelings and experiences helps us to form and develop our own ideas and beliefs.

At first, someone else may help us to do something which we are eventually able to do alone.

I DON'T KNOW WHY I HAVE TO GO TO SCHOOL. IT'S ALL SO BORING.

YOU'RE THE BORING ONE. YOU'RE ALWAYS MOANING ABOUT IT. YOU JUST CAN'T BE BOTHERED TO DO ANY WORK.

STOP ARGUING, YOU TWO. CLARE DOES HAVE A POINT, THOUGH, GREG. I CAN REMEMBER WHEN YOU USED TO LOOK FORWARD TO GOING TO SCHOOL.

△ Greg said that was years ago. School used to be fun then.

WELL, I HOPE YOU'LL FEEL DIFFERENTLY ABOUT MY LESSONS, GREG. DO GIVE US A CHANCE. YOU'VE ONLY JUST ARRIVED.

I THINK LESSONS ARE REALLY IMPORTANT. IF YOU DON'T LEARN THINGS, HOW CAN YOU KNOW ANYTHING?

△ Suddenly everyone wanted to put their point of view.

▽ John said Maria was just trying to impress Mr Kingsmill.

WHY DO YOU HAVE TO GO TO SCHOOL, THOUGH? YOU COULD LEARN WHAT YOU WANTED AT HOME. MY GRAN LEFT SCHOOL WHEN SHE WAS FOURTEEN. IT NEVER DID HER ANY HARM.

I SORT OF AGREE. I MEAN, YOU DO HAVE TO GO TO SCHOOL TO LEARN, BUT A LOT OF WHAT WE'RE TAUGHT HAS NOTHING TO DO WITH OUR LIVES.

▽ At school, the teacher, Mr Kingsmill, asked Greg to introduce himself to the class.

MY NAME'S GREG WELLS, AND I'VE JUST MOVED HERE WITH MY FAMILY. MY MUM'S AN ASSISTANT BANK MANAGER, AND SHE'S JUST BEEN PROMOTED. THAT'S WHY I HAVE TO START SCHOOL IN THE MIDDLE OF TERM. I HATED MY LAST SCHOOL, ANYWAY. IN FACT, I THINK LESSONS ARE A WASTE OF TIME.

IT'S OK FOR YOU, SHARON, YOU NEARLY ALWAYS DO WELL.

JOHN'S RIGHT. YOU PICK EVERYTHING UP REALLY QUICKLY. I LIKE SOME SUBJECTS, BUT I JUST DON'T SEE THE POINT OF OTHERS. I KNOW I'M NEVER GOING TO BE ANY GOOD AT THEM, SO WHY SHOULD I HAVE TO TAKE THEM?

HOW DO YOU KNOW YOU'RE NOT GOING TO BE ANY GOOD, THOUGH, KHALID? I USED TO HATE SCIENCE, BUT NOW IT'S MY FAVOURITE SUBJECT.

NOT NOW, MAYBE, BUT LATER ON IT CAN MAKE A DIFFERENCE. MY BROTHER, MIKE, HAS JUST GOT A NEW JOB, WHICH HE WOULDN'T HAVE GOT WITHOUT HIS MATHS QUALIFICATION.

SCHOOL'S NOT JUST ABOUT SUBJECTS AND QUALIFICATIONS. IT'S ALSO ABOUT LEARNING HOW TO GET ALONG WITH OTHER PEOPLE, AND WORKING OUT WHAT YOU WANT TO DO WITH YOUR LIFE.

△ They discussed the issue some more before the lesson continued.

TEACHERS ARE NOT THE ONLY INFLUENCE ON WHAT WE LEARN.

Not all learning takes place in school. We are constantly receiving opinions and information from friends, relatives, books and television. Often it is by watching and listening to others, that we are able to form our own views about situations.

JULIA DOESN'T SEE THE POINT OF SOME SCHOOLWORK.

It can be difficult to pick something up if you think that it will never be of any use to you. However, people's interests and outlooks often change with time. Things which are outside your experience now, may become significant to you later on.

WE ALL FIND SOME THINGS EASIER TO LEARN THAN OTHERS.

When you are having difficulty, it can be tempting to give up. As Maria said, some subjects take time to understand fully. This is why it is important to stick at things, and to ask questions. If you don't make sense of something immediately, it doesn't mean that you will never be able to learn it. We can all forget things or find it hard to pay attention. But constant difficulties with reading, writing and concentration can make the learning process very hard.

— 3 — Different Difficulties

People have difficulty with learning for all sorts of reasons, many of which are not related to their general level of ability. Like dyslexia, some of these problems have specific names. For example, extreme restlessness is called 'hyperactivity', and a constant inability to concentrate is called 'attention deficit disorder'. All these conditions can be obstacles to learning.

From time to time, we may all feel restless, have difficulty in following instructions or be clumsy. But this does not necessarily mean that we have a particular, persistent difficulty which gets in the way of our being able to do the things we otherwise feel we should be able to do. Sometimes, the way we feel about ourselves can also make learning things difficult. Some people assume that they will not succeed, and so they stop trying. The more you believe that you cannot do something, the more difficult it becomes to actually do it. A fear of making mistakes or being laughed at can put a lot of pressure on us. Other people's expectations may also affect our performance.

Poor eyesight can cause problems with learning but can quickly be corrected by the wearing of glasses. Dyslexia, hyperactivity or a lack of confidence also make learning hard. Unfortunately, there is no such quick solution to the difficulties created by such conditions and feelings.

▽ A couple of weeks later, Greg and his new friends were walking home from school.

I CAN'T BELIEVE MR KINGSMILL IS GOING TO GIVE US A TEST TOMORROW. IT'S NOT FAIR.

YOU ALWAYS SAY THAT. YOU'VE NOTHING TO WORRY ABOUT, ANYWAY. YOU'RE GOOD AT SCIENCE.

YES, YOU'RE A PROPER LITTLE SWOT. TESTS MAKE ME REALLY NERVOUS AND I FORGET THE ANSWERS.

THAT'S JUST YOUR EXCUSE, JULIA, TO COVER UP THE FACT THAT YOU'RE THICK.

YES. YOU'LL END UP LIKE YOUR BROTHER, ABEL. I HEARD HE STILL HAS TO READ KIDS' BOOKS, BECAUSE HE CAN'T READ PROPERLY YET. CAN YOU BELIEVE IT?

△ Sharon told Maria she was being really cruel.

▽ Greg said he wasn't looking forward to the test either.

YOU DON'T KNOW ANYTHING ABOUT MY BROTHER. NEITHER OF US IS THICK. BESIDES, I DON'T SEE YOU WINNING ANY CLASS PRIZES FOR BEING BRAINY.

TAKE NO NOTICE. THEY'RE JUST TRYING TO WIND YOU UP. THAT'S TYPICAL OF YOU TWO. ABEL'S REALLY NICE.

ANYWAY, IT'S SCIENCE. I DON'T SEE WHY WE SHOULD HAVE TO SIT A WRITTEN TEST IN SCIENCE. IT'S SUPPOSED TO BE PRACTICAL.

WHAT IS IT WITH YOU? YOU'RE ALWAYS MOANING ABOUT WORK. I'M GOING HOME TO REVISE. MAYBE YOU SHOULD DO THE SAME.

△ John and Maria said they were just joking, but Julia said she didn't find it funny.

▽ The next day, Greg was studying for the test. But he found reading and writing very difficult.

HOW ARE YOU GETTING ON, GREG? WOULD YOU LIKE ME TO TEST YOU?

NO, THAT'S OK, MUM. I'VE DONE ALL I NEED TO.

DON'T BELIEVE HIM, MUM. HE'S JUST BEEN SITTING THERE STARING AT THE SAME PAGE FOR AGES.

▽ Greg told Clare to mind her own business.

DON'T TALK TO YOUR SISTER LIKE THAT, GREG.

WHY DOES EVERYONE ALWAYS GET AT ME? IT'S OK FOR HER. JUST BECAUSE SHE'S SO PERFECT AT SCHOOL, SHE THINKS SHE KNOWS EVERYTHING.

▽ Greg left for school. He was really worried about the written test.

> I THINK I'VE FORGOTTEN EVERY-THING I'VE READ. IT'S ALWAYS LIKE THIS WITH ME. MY MEMORY'S TERRIBLE.

> I JUST WANT TO GET IT OVER WITH, NOW. I KNOW I'LL DO BADLY, ANYWAY.

▽ As Greg had feared, making sense of the questions was difficult. After the written test came the practical experiment.

> I'M SORRY. I CAN'T WORK OUT WHAT I'M DOING WRONG.

> YOU'VE DROPPED IT THREE TIMES ALREADY. WE'RE GOING TO BE HERE ALL DAY. LET ME DO IT. THIS EXPERIMENT COUNTS FOR HALF THE MARKS, YOU KNOW.

> GREAT, GREG, EXCEPT YOU'VE GOT IT ROUND THE WRONG WAY. CAN'T YOU TELL YOUR LEFT FROM YOUR RIGHT?

> I'LL SORT IT OUT. COME ON, YOU LOT, TIME'S RUNNING OUT. WHO'S GOING TO RECORD THE RESULTS?

△ Greg took the equipment from Khalid, and quickly assembled it.

△ Greg suggested John should be the one to write down what happened during the experiment.

▽ That evening at home, Sharon's mum asked her how she thought the test had gone.

> THINK I DID OK. THERE RE SOME PARTS OF THE RITTEN TEST WHERE I T COULDN'T REMEMBER NGS. I REVISE AND REVISE D I THINK I KNOW IT, BUT EN IT ALL SEEMS TO GO, ST WHEN IT MATTERS ST.

> I WOULDN'T WORRY TOO MUCH, DARLING. YOU'RE JUST TRYING TO TAKE IN A LOT OF NEW INFORMATION.

▽ Sharon's brother Mike came in saying that he'd failed his driving test.

> OH, MIKE. I'M SORRY. AND I WAS SO SURE YOU WERE GOING TO PASS.

> SO WAS I. I JUST PANICKED. I'D PLANNED TO GO OUT WITH MY MATES TONIGHT, TOO, TO CELEBRATE.

JOHN AND MARIA HAVE SAID UNKIND THINGS ABOUT JULIA AND ABEL.
Words like 'thick', often said as a joke, can be very hurtful. Sometimes they are used so often that people forget just how nasty they are. Labelling people in this way is not helpful. It focuses only on what you assume people cannot do, rather than stressing what they can do.

INTELLIGENCE IS DIFFICULT TO MEASURE.
Julia knows that a difficulty with learning, such as a poor memory or clumsiness, does not necessarily mean that a person is less intelligent than someone else. Those with a problem might take longer to learn something but this is not the same as lacking intelligence. People who have difficulty learning certain things may be good at others. People who are dyslexic or hyperactive are often very bright. It is important not to jump to conclusions about people.

THE STRESS OF A SITUATION CAN AFFECT HOW WELL WE PERFORM.
This is one reason why people like Julia find tests and exams difficult. We can do the work and know the answers, but the anxiety about being 'on the spot' can seem to blot out everything else. Learning how to relax and cope with this situation is a skill that can be developed. Worrying about problems we are having with a subject can add to the difficulty and pressure that we feel.

What Is Dyslexia?

The word dyslexia comes from Greek and means 'difficulty with words'. Today, dyslexia describes a condition in which people have specific difficulties with reading, writing and spelling. It includes similar problems with number work and recognising symbols, such as musical notes or mathematical signs. Dyslexia can cause clumsiness, poor concentration and memory problems.

Someone with dyslexia may read or write words and numbers the wrong way round. Another may see shapes and blurs when reading. It can be very hard for people with dyslexia to spell words or form letters.

Dyslexia affects people from all backgrounds, races and ages. It is not a disease and cannot be passed from one child to another. It is believed that dyslexia is a condition which is most often passed down from parent to child. Everybody's brain is unique, but research has shown that the brains of people with dyslexia seem to use different pathways to organise information. The severity of symptoms will vary from person to person. The difficulties caused by dyslexia can cause great anxiety and upset. Dyslexia is not something you grow out of, but there are techniques which can be learnt to help cope with the problems.

▽ Mr Kingsmill gave the class their test results the next morning.

YOU DID EVEN WORSE THAN I DID.

I JUST COULDN'T BE BOTHERED WITH THE TEST, THAT'S ALL. I HAD THINGS ON MY MIND. I DIDN'T HAVE TIME TO REVISE.

WHAT IS THAT WRITING, SOME KIND OF CODE?

YES, IT'S CODE FOR MIND YOUR OWN BUSINESS.

HOW DID YOU DO, ANYWAY? I SUPPOSE YOU GOT GOOD GRADES AS USUAL.

△ As the others discussed their marks, Greg felt relieved not to be the centre of attention any more.

▽ A few weeks later, in English class, it was Greg's turn to read in front of the class.

THAT'S THE WRONG PLACE, GREG.

YOU'VE SKIPPED A CHAPTER, DUMMY. WE'RE ONLY UP TO CHAPTER FOUR.

DON'T WORRY, GREG. JUST GO BACK AND START FROM WHERE WE FINISHED LAST TIME.

WHAT'S TAKING HIM SO LONG? IS HIS READING AS BAD AS HIS WRITING?

LEAVE HIM ALONE. WHY ARE YOU ALWAYS SO NASTY?

I'M SICK OF EVERYONE PICKING ON ME ALL THE TIME. I HATE READING, AND I'M NOT GOING TO DO IT.

▽ Greg was horrified. He'd worked so hard to learn his chapter. He felt embarrassed and upset.

I DON'T WANT TO READ THAT STUPID BOOK, ANYWAY!

GREG, COME BACK HERE.

▷ Greg ran out of the classroom.

▽ That evening, Mr and Mrs Wells confronted Greg.

THE SCHOOL PHONED TODAY. THEY SAID YOU'D STORMED OUT OF CLASS IN THE MIDDLE OF A LESSON.

YOUR TEACHER, MR BROOKES, HAS ASKED US TO GO IN TO SEE HIM. JUST WHAT IS GOING ON, GREG?

MARIA CAME UP TO ME TODAY AT SCHOOL - SHE'S IN GREG'S CLASS. SHE SAID HE SHOUTED AT THE TEACHER AND THREW HIS BOOK ACROSS THE ROOM.

MARIA'S JUST A TELL-TALE. SHE LOVES TO GET PEOPLE INTO TROUBLE. WHO ASKED FOR YOUR OPINION, ANYWAY?

△ Clare and Greg began to argue.

CALM DOWN, YOU TWO. GREG, WE JUST DON'T UNDERSTAND WHAT'S WRONG WITH YOU LATELY. THIS ISN'T THE FIRST TIME YOU'VE BEEN IN TROUBLE.

SO WHAT? I DON'T CARE.

I DON'T BELIEVE YOU, GREG.

YOU CAN'T GO ON LIKE THIS, SON. WHAT'S WRONG?

◁ Greg ran upstairs to his room. Later, Clare came up to talk to him.

I JUST CAN'T DO IT, THAT'S WHAT'S WRONG. I KEEP TRYING TO TELL YOU, BUT NOBODY BELIEVES ME. YOU ALL JUST KEEP TELLING ME HOW WELL CLARE'S DOING, AND THAT I NEED TO WORK HARDER.

LOOK, I'M SORRY ABOUT EARLIER.

IT'S ALL RIGHT FOR YOU. JUST BECAUSE I'M NOT DOING AS BRILLIANTLY AS YOU AT SCHOOL, I'M THE ONE WHO GETS TOLD OFF ALL THE TIME.

△ Greg had begun to believe that he was simply less intelligent than the others in his class.

However,bytheend   oftheday hehad decidedthat this schoolwasbetter   than the last oneeventhough he didn'tlikeit.   Nobodyhad   offeredto pullhishead off,riphiscoat   orthrow   hisshoes overtheroof. on theotherhand,   nobody   hadspoken   tohimeither By Thursdayafter noon,   nothinghad   changedBill was notentirely surprisednoonespoke tohimbecause no oneknewhewas thereeverydayhewas witanother group.   Heonly sawhisclasstogether atergridtime after thatthey   weresplitupforall   theirlessons. Maths withlx Englishwithlcgames   with2yalesson which   was   mysteriouslycalled   GSwithlz.Atthe endof   that   periodhewasnowiser   aboutGSthanhehad been atthe   beginning,Itseemed   thatthe classwas on   page135 ofbook2whilethe teacherwas   onpage 135 ofbook   3asbothbookshad   identical   covers the lesson   wasoverbeforeany   onenoticed Billhad had nobook   anywaybeingadvised   toshare   withaboy in   apink   shirtwhokepthiselbow   firmly between

We all see thing the same way. We see words in groups or phrases. The print is more dominant than the background. The print shows no movement. The printed letters are evenly black. Black print on white paper gives the best contrast for everyone. White background looks white.

ing comprehension, reading accuracy, but not in rate of reading. Adler and Atwood (1987) evaluated the results of Irlen Lenses on 23 remedial high school students and a matched control group. Significant improvement for the experimental group was noted for time needed to locate words on a printed page, timed reading scores, length of time for sustained reading, and span of focus, as well as other perceptual tasks. Additionally, seven of the 23 experimental found employment, but none of the control group was employed by the end of the semester.

In contrast, Winters (1987) was unable to find differences in his study. Winters gave 15 elementary school children four minutes to locate and circle 68 examples of the letter

GREG IS FEELING VERY ANGRY AND UPSET.

Having a difficulty which gets in the way of your general ability to do things can make you feel very unhappy. Some people feel that the whole world is against them and that nobody understands them. Young people might express their feelings by becoming withdrawn or throwing tantrums. Some people with dyslexia try to avoid situations in which they have to read or write. Or, like Greg, they may try to hide their difficulty. Others play truant or pretend to be ill. But this does not solve anything. No one should be afraid to admit that they have a problem and ask for help.

FACTFILE: TYPICAL DIFFICULTIES

These are some typical problems dyslexics may have when reading, writing or spelling:

- Seeing words and letters as strange shapes or blurs, as shown above and left.
- Reading 'a' for 'and' or 'from' for 'for'.
- Swapping letters – 'aminal' for 'animal'.
- Inverting letters (putting them the wrong way round) – 'u' for 'n' or 'w' for 'm'.
- Mirror writing and reversing letters – 'b' for 'd'.
- Omitting letters – 'tie' for 'time'.
- Adding letters – 'whin' for 'win'.
- Spellings which don't agree with the sound of the word, such as 'please' – 'pley'.

It is important to remember that some of these mistakes are very common. Just because you make one or more of these, does not necessarily mean you are dyslexic.

−5− Recognising Dyslexia

Up to one in ten children has some form of dyslexia. It is recognised in more boys than girls.

It is important that dyslexia is identified as early as possible. The more quickly specialist help is given, the easier it will be for a young person to cope. But dyslexia is not always easy to spot. Many young children make similar mistakes to young people who are dyslexic. However, dyslexia can often be identified by the severity of any symptoms and the length of time over which they persist.

Dyslexic children are often very bright and able to express their ideas well in discussions. They are often very artistic and creative and can be particularly good at operating equipment, such as computers.

A family history of dyslexia and having speech problems as a toddler are important signs of dyslexia. Dyslexics often take longer to learn to speak clearly and to walk than others of the same age. They might also jumble up words and be poor at rhymes. Their reading may be slow and unsure, with words or sentences missed out. Writing might take a long time and be difficult to read, with smudges and little, if any, use of punctuation. Dyslexics may often have difficulty sorting right from left or telling the time.

▽ Two days later, Greg's parents went to see his English teacher, Mr Brookes.

WE'VE ASKED YOU TO COME IN BECAUSE WE'RE WORRIED ABOUT GREG'S PERFORMANCE, PARTICULARLY HIS WRITTEN WORK AND HIS BEHAVIOUR IN CLASS.

I'M AFRAID THERE WERE PROBLEMS AT HIS LAST SCHOOL. WE'VE TRIED TO TALK TO HIM, BUT HE JUST REFUSES TO LISTEN.

HE KEEPS SAYING THAT SCHOOL'S BORING AND A WASTE OF TIME. DEEP DOWN, I'M SURE HE DOESN'T BELIEVE THAT. HE USED TO LOVE GOING TO SCHOOL.

IN MANY WAYS, HE'S A VERY BRIGHT BOY. HE'S ALWAYS KEEN TO JOIN IN CLASS DISCUSSIONS, WHICH IS WHY WE THINK THE PROBLEM IS NOT JUST ABOUT HIS BEHAVIOUR.

△ Mr Brookes said they thought Greg might be dyslexic.

MR BROOKES, I'M SLIGHTLY DYSLEXIC MYSELF. WHEN I REALISED GREG HAD A PROBLEM, I ASKED THE TEACHERS AT HIS LAST SCHOOL IF THAT COULD BE THE REASON. THEY SAID NO.

THEY SAID HE WASN'T DYSLEXIC, JUST DIFFICULT. THEY SAID HIS WORK WAS SUFFERING BECAUSE HE WAS LAZY.

I DIDN'T FIND OUT I HAD A PROBLEM UNTIL I WAS TWENTY. I FELT ASHAMED OF IT. I WAS SO PLEASED TO BE TOLD THAT GREG WASN'T DYSLEXIC, I DIDN'T THINK TO QUESTION IT ANY MORE.

DYSLEXIA CAN GIVE OUT CONFUSING SIGNALS. IT'S SOMETIMES NOT EASY TO SPOT WHERE THE REAL PROBLEM IS. AND SOME CHILDREN ARE VERY GOOD AT COVERING UP THE FACT THAT THEY HAVE A PROBLEM AT ALL.

△ Mrs Wells said she felt guilty. She should have made more of a fuss.

▽ Greg came in. Mr Brookes explained that it was important Greg was assessed properly.

THIS IS NOTHING TO DO WITH CLEVERNESS, GREG.

WE HAVE TO MAKE SU[RE] YOU GET THE RIGHT K[IND] OF HELP.

◁ Greg wa[s] pleased he was being taken serio[usly] but he was worried abo[ut] what the othe[r] kids would say.

I'M SORRY, GREG, WE SHOULD HAVE REALISED BEFORE. WHY WOULDN'T YOU TALK TO US?

I DID TRY. BUT I FELT EMBARRASSED. I DIDN'T UNDERSTAND WHY I COULDN'T DO WHAT EVERYONE ELSE WAS DOING. IN THE END, I JUST THOUGHT I WAS STUPID.

MR BROOKES KNOWS HOW IMPORTANT IT IS THAT GREG IS PROPERLY ASSESSED TO MAKE CERTAIN HE IS DYSLEXIC.

Testing is important. Young people often show some of the signs of dyslexia, without necessarily being dyslexic. Sometimes parents may incorrectly label a child as dyslexic as a way of explaining poor performance. Usually, the more noticeable the symptoms, the easier the problem is to recognise. Being open with people about any worries can help to spot a problem early on. When the difficulty has been correctly identified, the best help can be found, whatever the problem.

CASE STUDY:
LOUIS, AGED 12

"I loved listening to stories in class but hated having to write anything down. It took me ages to finish any work, I'd get so embarrassed, because everyone else had finished and I'd hardly started. Reading was hard, too. I couldn't make sense of the words on the page. I knew something was wrong, but didn't know what. I still have some problems, but since my teachers found out I was dyslexic I've started going to special classes which really help. My reading is much better and my writing is getting clearer."

GREG HAD A REPUTATION FOR BEING A TROUBLE-MAKER.

People with dyslexia often know something is wrong, without fully understanding what it is. Their frustration may be expressed through disruptive behaviour. There is a danger that if parents or teachers focus only on the behaviour, they may not recognise what is causing it.

—6— Attitudes Towards Dyslexia And Other Difficulties

Dyslexia and similar difficulties can present young people with both practical and emotional hurdles. These can be hard to overcome. Some people with a learning problem find the situation is made worse because they have to deal not only with their learning difficulty, but also with the unhelpful attitudes of others towards them.

Not being able to remember things, or being very clumsy can obviously affect the way you feel about yourself. But because these difficulties do not have specific labels, some people dismiss their importance.

It can be very hurtful if someone else makes fun of a problem that you are fighting to solve. People with dyslexia are sometimes the target of bullying or teasing. Despite the fact that they are often working very hard, many people with a learning difficulty have been called lazy or stupid, or made to feel like failures. Sometimes even parents may not fully understand and feel embarrassed that their child has a learning problem. Or they may make light of it in front of others. Some parents try to offer too much help, adding to the pressure to do well. But this does not always help the young person.

▽ The next day, Greg's friends all wanted to know what had happened.

▽ His friends wouldn't leave him alone. Eventually, Greg told them Mr Brookes thought he might be dyslexic.

DID YOU GET INTO TROUBLE?

OH, YOU'D REALLY LIKE THAT, WOULDN'T YOU?

I DIDN'T, AS A MATTER OF FACT. I DON'T REALLY WANT TO TALK ABOUT IT.

WHAT DOES THAT MEAN, ANYWAY?

IT MEANS HAVING PROBLEMS WITH READING AND WRITING AND STUFF LIKE THAT.

MY DAD SAYS THERE'S NO SUCH THING. IT'S JUST AN EXCUSE TO COVER UP THE FACT THAT SOMEONE'S STUPID.

SAYING THAT IS THE ONLY THING THAT'S STUPID. LOTS OF PEOPLE HAVE DYSLEXIA, AND IT'S NOTHING TO DO WITH INTELLIGENCE.

THAT'S RIGHT. SO WHAT HAPPENS NOW, GREG?

▽ It was several months later. The school had arranged specialist teaching for Greg. He was making progress with his teacher, Malcolm.

THIS IS REALLY GOOD, GREG.

THANKS. IT'S STILL TAKING ME A WHILE TO GET IT RIGHT, BUT I'VE STOPPED MAKING SOME OF THE OLD MISTAKES.

△ Greg told them that first he would be tested.
▽ One evening, Julia asked Greg how things were.

E-THINGS ARE MUCH BETTER N. JOHN AND MARIA STILL MAKE MARKS ABOUT ME BEING THICK D STUFF, BUT I DON'T TAKE ANY TICE OF THEM.

THEY STILL MAKE COMMENTS ABOUT MY BROTHER, TOO. HE HAS SOMETHING CALLED 'ATTENTION DEFICIT DISORDER,' WHICH MEANS HE HAS PROBLEMS LEARNING THINGS, AS WELL.

PEOPLE DON'T UNDERSTAND. I DIDN'T MYSELF AT FIRST. I THOUGHT I WAS THE ONLY ONE WITH A PROBLEM. FINDING OUT THAT THERE WERE OTHERS IN THE SAME SITUATION REALLY HELPED. NOW I DON'T FEEL EMBARRASSED ANY MORE.

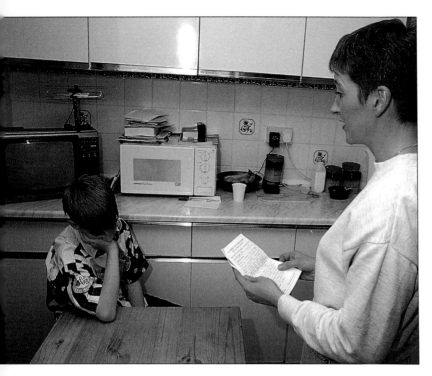

FOR YEARS, PEOPLE DID NOT BELIEVE THAT DYSLEXIA ACTUALLY EXISTED.

Like John's father, they assumed that the claims young people made about problems with reading and writing were excuses for laziness, lack of intelligence or bad behaviour. Unfortunately, it is an attitude some people still express today. This is why everyone needs to be aware of the very real nature of dyslexia, hyperactivity and attention deficit disorder, and to understand how they can affect people's lives. Because of this, it is important not to hide any difficulties you may have from parents or teachers.

OUR DIFFERENCES ARE SOMETHING THAT WE SHOULD ALL WELCOME, RATHER THAN DISMISS.

There is no such thing as a 'normal' person. There are all sorts of people with all kinds of strengths and levels of ability in the world. Everyone is unique.

GREG NOW RECEIVES SPECIALIST TEACHING.

Once dyslexia has been officially recognised, schools have a duty to provide help. Most will do their best to make sure a child's needs are met, but it is not always easy to secure the right treatment. It can be expensive. Individual tuition from a special-ist will often be of most help.

How Are People Affected?

"At first I was relieved that I was being taken seriously. Then I became worried about how people would react. But it's been okay."

The effect of dyslexia and associated difficulties on a person's life will depend on the kind of problem she or he has, and how severe it is. The attitude of others will also play a part, as will the support a person receives in dealing with the difficulty. Once a diagnosis has been made, it is important that people not only deal with the specific problem, but also focus on the person's strengths.

At times, it may seem as if the extra work you need to do is never-ending. If you do get very tired, tell your parents or carers.

If a condition has been unrecognised for a long time, the young person may have become ashamed of it. This can have an effect on the person's sense of worth in other areas of her or his life. Some people come to believe that they are failures or feel misunderstood. This can lead to other problems, such as aggression or loneliness. Someone who is hyperactive may also find it difficult to get on with classmates. Some people resent being labelled as dyslexic, particularly if their symptoms are mild. Severe dyslexia can influence the choice of job which is available, but nobody should make assumptions. The future will depend on a person's progress and ability to cope with the condition.

How Are People Affected?

▽ Greg and his friends were all going to be in the school play at the end of term.

▽ Greg said he was having to do a lot of hard work, and he resented it sometimes.

▽ The next day, Greg was doing his homework in the living room.

△ Clare went upstairs to her room. Later, her mum came up to see her.

△ Mrs Wells told Clare that everyone was still really proud of her.

OVERCOMING A DIFFICULTY SUCH AS DYSLEXIA MAY INVOLVE A LOT OF HARD WORK AND EFFORT.

This can be frustrating and very tiring at times, especially if you have to attend extra classes. You may feel resentful if you see your friends out enjoying themselves, while you are still working. There might even be times when you feel like giving up. However, the sense of achievement you feel when you have worked especially hard at something, can be very satisfying.

CLARE RESENTS THE FUSS BEING MADE OF GREG.

If you have a sister or brother who is dyslexic, you might think it is unfair that he or she seems to be getting all the attention. However, you may feel guilty about feeling that way. Or you may be upset that you can do things which a close friend finds hard. These are quite natural emotions.

**CASE STUDY:
DAVID, AGED 21**

"When I was younger, I always wanted to be a writer. But the others just laughed at me because my reading and spelling were so bad. Luckily, my parents realised early on that something was wrong. I had special classes for dyslexia, and had to work really hard. Even though my family and friends were really understanding, sometimes I felt like giving up – it seemed like I'd never be able to do it. But it was worth it. I've just got a job writing a feature for a magazine. It'll mean a lot of work, but I'm used to that."

Living With Dyslexia

"I've made a lot of new friends since I found out I was dyslexic. Many of them have similar problems. It's made me realise that dyslexia is nothing to be ashamed of."

There is no cure for dyslexia, but there are ways in which the problems can be reduced. With the right teaching and support, reading and writing can improve greatly. Not all people with dyslexia experience the same problems; they will not all need exactly the same help. Specialist teaching can help people to cope with their particular difficulties and find ways of overcoming them.

Young people with dyslexia will often benefit from some specialist individual tuition. They may then be able to learn more confidently in a larger class.

Living with dyslexia means coping both with the practical difficulties it causes and coming to terms with the way it makes you feel. It is important for someone who is dyslexic or has another difficulty not to lose patience. These problems can be very frustrating but there are ways of dealing with them. There is no need to feel ashamed or angry. It can help to talk about your feelings instead of bottling them up. Support from friends and family can also be important. If you know of someone with a difficulty, you should be sensitive to that person's needs, and know when it is most useful to offer assistance and when it is not. Some people may be grateful for help. Others may wish to do things for themselves.

▽ One day at school, John and Khalid came across Greg, Christopher and Aysha in the school corridor.

> HI, GUYS. READ ANY GOOD BOOKS LATELY?

> VERY FUNNY.

> AS A MATTER OF FACT, I HAVE. IT WAS A BOOK ALL ABOUT DYSLEXIA, ACTUALLY.

> BEING DYSLEXIC DOESN'T MAKE YOU STUPID. NOT UNLESS YOU'D CALL PEOPLE LIKE ALBERT EINSTEIN STUPID. IT JUST GOES TO SHOW HOW LITTLE YOU KNOW.

> HE'S RIGHT, JOHN—LOTS OF FAMOUS PEOPLE ARE DYSLEXIC.

△ John left, feeling slightly embarrassed. Khalid followed him.

▽ It was the last week of term. Greg and Sharon were waiting to go on in the play.

> PEOPLE CAN BE REALLY CRUEL. I SOMETIMES THINK IT WAS BETTER BEFORE, WHEN NOBODY KNEW ABOUT IT.

> I KNOW IT'S DIFFICULT HAVING TO GO TO EXTRA LESSONS AND DIFFERENT CLASSES, BUT I'M STILL GLAD I FOUND OUT. OTHERWISE I'D HAVE GONE ON WONDERING WHY I COULDN'T DO THE WORK AND THINKING I WAS STUPID.

> I HOPE I REMEMBER EVERYTHING. THAT BOOK WAS GREAT, BY THE WAY. I'M STILL NERVOUS, THOUGH.

> ME TOO, BUT I'M SURE WE'LL BE FINE.

△ Aysha agreed with Greg, really, but said she still felt embarrassed sometimes.

> I'M GLAD I DIDN'T LET THEM GET THE BETTER OF ME.

> I ALMOST GAVE UP AT ONE POINT. JOHN AND MARIA JUST LAUGHED WHEN I TOLD THEM I WAS GOING TO BE IN THE PLAY. THEY THOUGHT I WOULDN'T BE ABLE TO DO IT. THEY SAID IT SO OFTEN I ALMOST BEGAN TO BELIEVE IT MYSELF.

> YOU'RE A REALLY GOOD ACTOR. COME ON, LET'S SHOW THEM WHAT WE CAN DO.

△ The two of them went on stage.

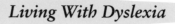

SHARON AND GREG HAVE BEEN A GREAT SUCCESS IN THE SCHOOL PLAY.

People with dyslexia can excel in many fields, even where reading, writing, diagrams and responding to instructions are important. The great scientist Michael Faraday and the poet W.B. Yeats were dyslexic, as is the film star Tom Cruise. Dyslexia need not be a barrier to your success or happiness.

AYSHA WAS UPSET BY OTHERS' COMMENTS.

Receiving help for dyslexia is important, but it can make you feel singled out. If you are teased, the feelings this can leave you with can be difficult to handle. But remember that dyslexia is nothing to be embarrassed about.

CASE STUDY:
PAUL, AGED 12

"I found out I was dyslexic when I was nine. I went to special classes to help me with my reading and writing. When I started I couldn't spell even simple words. I never used full stops or commas. I didn't like to read, because everything seemed jumbled up on the page. The teachers showed me how to shape letters properly. Word games and listening to tapes helped me to understand how what you read and how it all sounds is connected. I can now read and write much better. Knowing that my problems had nothing to do with being less clever than anyone else, has made me feel a lot better about myself."

Other Ways Of Coping

"For me, one of the things which helped most was having my problem taken seriously by people who really understood it."

The more that is known about any difficulty such as dyslexia, and the earlier it is identified, the easier it is likely to be for the person to receive the help she or he needs. Many people agree that education can play a large role in this, helping us both to recognise the signs of a problem and to make sure that people understand fully the nature of the difficulties.

A wide range of support is available to help people cope with dyslexia and other difficulties. This might be from speech therapists, doctors, or teachers who are aware of the special educational needs of some young people.

Good teachers know that we all learn in different ways, and will vary the way that they teach to take this into account. They also know when it's appropriate to give someone time to think things through alone. Class teachers may allow extra time to complete tasks or leave information on a board or overhead projector. Extra time may be given for tests and exams. Practical ways of helping with reading and writing might include borrowing notes which a friend has made. Some people use a tape recorder and make notes themselves later. If you have a very bad memory, it can help to write out lists or check that you have everything prepared that you will need for the next day at school.

Other Ways Of Coping

▽ It was the summer holidays. Greg had invited some friends round one afternoon.

IT'S A KIND OF EARLY BIRTHDAY PRESENT. IT WILL HELP ME TO DO MY WORK. IT'S ALSO GOT A CD ROM AND SPEAKER ATTACHMENT.

HE'S PROMISED I CAN USE IT, TOO. I PLAN TO HOLD HIM TO THAT.

HOW ARE YOU AND CLARE GETTING ALONG NOW? STILL HAVING PROBLEMS?

WE STILL ARGUE SOMETIMES, USUALLY WHEN I GET FRUSTRATED AT NOT BEING ABLE TO DO SOMETHING, BUT IT'S NOT SO BAD, NOW.

MUM'S STOPPED FUSSING SO MUCH, TOO. SHE FELT REALLY GUILTY, I THINK, BECAUSE SHE THOUGHT SHE SHOULD HAVE KNOWN I WAS DYSLEXIC EARLIER ON. BUT IT'S NOT HER FAULT. SHE'S WORRIED ABOUT PAMELA, THOUGH, IN CASE SHE TURNS OUT TO BE DYSLEXIC.

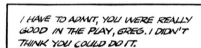

I HAVE TO ADMIT, YOU WERE REALLY GOOD IN THE PLAY, GREG. I DIDN'T THINK YOU COULD DO IT.

THANKS. SHARON WAS GOOD, TOO, WASN'T SHE? AND WITHOUT ANY PROMPTING EITHER!

△ John and Sharon came over to join them both.

I KNOW. I WAS REALLY PLEASED. LOOK, I'VE GOT TO GO. I'M MEETING MIKE. HE'S FINALLY PASSED HIS DRIVING TEST, AND HE'S TAKING US ALL OUT FOR THE DAY.

△ Sharon left. The others went back to the computer.

YOU'VE PICKED THIS UP REALLY QUICKLY.

I THINK GREG KNOWS MORE ABOUT COMPUTERS THAN MALCOLM.

NO I DON'T, BUT I'M HAVING FUN LEARNING.

LEARNING TO COPE WITH ANY DIFFICULTY CAN TAKE TIME, AND THERE MAY BE SETBACKS.

From time to time, you might feel angry or resentful that you have to work so hard. You may sometimes feel as if things will never change. Sometimes it may seem as if you take two steps forward and then one step back. Progress takes time. Putting up with unfair comments from other people can be hard too, but it is important not to let any of this affect your expectations of yourself.

ONE WAY IN WHICH EVERYONE CAN HELP IS BY NOT GIVING IN TO PREJUDICE.

Every person is different. Society would be very boring indeed if we were all the same. Understanding and challenging both your own prejudices and those of other people can help to stop differences being seen as wrong or undesirable. Each of us has something to offer and we can all learn from each other.

FACTFILE: PRACTICAL HELP

Other practical measures to help include:

- Specially adapted equipment – for example, finger grips, triangular pencils and sloped writing surfaces.
- Using computers and word processors.
- Spellcheckers and grammar checking programmes on computers.
- 'Speaking' computers and CD Roms
- Talking books (tapes) with text provided; dictation machines.
- Use of tape recorders to record information.
- Copying notes from a friend.
- Keeping a homework and study diary.

What Can We Do?

"A supportive teacher and family is as helpful as the special equipment at school."

Dyslexia and similar learning difficulties present young people with many challenges. Some of these will need a lot of patience and hard work to overcome. Having read this book, you will understand that there is much that can be done to lessen the problems. You will know the effects that learning difficulties can have on people's lives.

The right help and support from family, teachers and friends can make it much easier for a young person to cope with a learning difficulty.

Anybody can be affected by a difficulty with learning. It is not something to be ashamed of, nor is it something that others should make fun of. If you are worried about any aspect of your learning, talking to someone you trust about how you feel, and what your particular difficulties are, can help to make sure you receive any help you may need. Adults also need to be aware of potential problems, and need to know how to recognise the signs of conditions such as dyslexia. It is very important not to delay asking for specialist help if you think that it could be necessary.

Adults and children who have read this book together may like to discuss their feelings and talk about the issues involved. Anybody who would like to talk to someone else about dyslexia or other associated learning difficulties should be able to receive information, advice or support from the organisations listed below.

LADDER
The Learning, Hyperactivity and Attention Deficit Disorders Association
PO Box 700
Wolverhampton
WV3 7YY
Send a stamped addressed envelope for further information.

BRITISH DYSLEXIA ASSOCIATION
98 London Road
Reading
Berks
RG1 5AU
Tel: 0118 966 2677
Helpline: 0118 966 8271
E-mail:
info@dyslexia-bda.demon.co.uk
Website:
www.bda-dyslexia.org.uk

SCOTTISH DYSLEXIA ASSOCIATION
Unit 3, Stirling Business Centre
Wellgreen Place
Stirling FK8 2DZ
Tel: 01786 446650

MID-WALES DYSLEXIA GROUP
Tel: 01970 832559

NORTHERN IRELAND DYSLEXIA ASSOCIATION
Tel: 01265 329167
Helpline: 01232 243100

DYSLEXIA INSTITUTE
133 Gresham Road
Staines, Middlesex TW18 2AJ
Tel: 01784 463 851
E-mail:
info@dyslexia-inst.org.uk
Website:
www.dyslexia-inst.org.uk

DEPARTMENT OF HEALTH
Richmond House
79 Whitehall
London SW1A 2NS
Tel: 0800 665544 (health information service)
Tel: 0800 555777 (health literature line)

DYSLEXIA-SPELD FOUNDATION WA (Inc)
PO Box 409
South Perth
WA 6951
Australia
Tel: 00 619 367 3494

SPELD CANTERBURY (Inc)
PO Box 13 391
Armagh
Christchurch
New Zealand
Tel: 00 643 366 6430

Index

Picture Credits The publishers wish to acknowledge that all the people photographed in this book are models. All the pictures in this book are by Roger Vlitos apart from pages 6 top, page 23 top, page 24, page 26 bottom, page 30: Robert Harding; page 10, bottom, page 26 top: Frank Spooner; page 14 - pictures of how reading appears to individuals with visual dyslexia/Irlen Syndrome reproduced from Reading By The Colors by Helen Irlen, Avery Press, New York. Color treatment with Irlen Colored Filters helps dyslexia. 71 Irlen Centres worldwide. References included in Irlen's book or write Irlen Institute, 5380 Village Road, Long Beach CA 90808, USA Tel: 310 496 2550.